Your Journey to Fulfillment

ALSO BY HAMID SAFAEI

First-Class Leadership

*How Highly Effective Teams Can
Achieve Breakthrough Results*

Your Journey to Fulfillment

A Step-by-Step Guide to Realizing Your Dream

Hamid Safaei

ImOcean Academy
Unleash your potential!

Your Journey to Fulfillment

Copyright © 2017 by Hamid Safaei

2nd edition

Because of the dynamic nature of the Internet, any Web addresses or links contained in this book may have changed since publication and may no longer be valid. The views expressed in this work are solely those of the author and do not necessarily reflect those of the publisher. While the publisher and author have used their best efforts in preparing this book, they make no representations or warranties with respect to the accuracy or

For bulk orders please contact
info@imocean.academy

Author: Hamid Safaei
Title: Your Journey to Fulfillment
Subtitle: A Step-by-Step Guide to Realizing
Your Dream
ISBN: 9781549694752
Category: SELF-HELP/ COACHING/
GENERAL
Published by: ImOcean Academy
Edited by: A Scribing Hand
Images by: Getty Images

info@imocean.academy

Cell: +31614288114 - Fixed: +31207749765

Korenbloemlaan 74, 1187 EG Amstelveen,

The Netherlands

Dedication

To my mother, who has been the greatest symbol of perseverance throughout her seven years fighting cancer.

To my father, my role model for resourcefulness from whom I learned to live a fruitful life based on the purest principles and values.

To my lovely wife Azadeh, who has unconditionally supported me through thick and thin.

To my son Arwin, a great source of inspiration who amazes me every day with his high rate of curiosity and unconditional love.

Contents

De-stress Your Mind and Body 71

Final word 93

Gifts for you 98

Introduction

Consider this book as my contribution to achieving your goals. I believe when people are happy, fulfilled, and satisfied there will be in general more peace, compassion, mutual understanding, and respect. This can only happen when we have more happy people in the room rather than grumpy, exhausted, unsatisfied, stressed, and aggressive ones. Think about it for a minute. Where do all those unpleasant feelings come from? Would it be fair to say that it happened due to the fact that we realize we haven't achieved what we wanted? Or even worse, we might be spending too much time doing things other than what we really want to do. Sound familiar?

Have you ever spent quality time asking yourself questions like: *"What do I really want?"*, *"Why is it never enough?"*, *"When will this all come to an end?"*, *"When can I smile again from the bottom of my heart?"* Have you also asked yourself why you are stuck, if you are? Have you learned from past successes using these as a template to achieve more?

Have you ever thought: "*If only I had a coach.*", "*I wish I had a guide, a template, a role model or someone who could tell me how to start.*"

I have good news for you my friend. I have put my top tips together to help you start realizing your dreams. I have learned to live the life I love from great people, great leaders, and beautiful souls. My parents never went to school. Yet they have been the best parents I could ever have had. By following their wisdom, I am where I am today. I have learned how to achieve financial freedom. Don't confuse financial freedom with having so much money that you don't need any more. I have learned to release myself from working for money. I have learned to follow my heart no matter how hard it is. I have learned to say no to scary leaders who are bad losers and all they want to hear is: "*Yes sir, you're right*". I have freed myself from many man-made obstacles. And I believe you deserve it too. Why not you?

I have penned this book to help you on your journey to ultimate success. This book is written in very simple language enabling you to start realizing your dreams. If you follow the guidelines outlined in this book you will make breakthroughs you never dared to imagine. The goal-setting exercises will move you from a passive to a resourceful state and breakthrough your limiting beliefs. Follow these bulletproof steps and you will realize your dreams in no time. All you need is yourself, your time and your commitment to act.

I would love to hear your story. Please connect with me on Facebook, LinkedIn, Instagram and Twitter. When you have realized your dream, please let me know how this book contributed to that. If you like what you read please leave a review on Amazon. Please be generous and pass on your knowledge. You can't imagine how many souls are waiting to be transformed by your knowledge and wisdom. See you at the top.

Chapter 1

The Best Version of Yourself

"Everybody is a genius. But if you judge a fish by its ability to climb a tree, it will live its whole life believing that it is stupid."~ Albert Einstein

Be the best version of yourself

How often have you found yourself asking the following questions?

- "I can do better. Why am I still doing this job?"
- "Don't I deserve better?"
- "When will this end?"

The better questions to ask might be:

- "Do I know what I want to achieve?"
- "Have I done anything to attain this?"
- "What am I capable of doing on my own?"
- "How can I be the best version of myself?"
- "Who can help me accelerate?"

I'd like to share the following thoughts which I believe will help you unlock your full potential.

1.1. Change is inevitable

Charles Robert Darwin said: "*It is not the strongest of the species that survive, nor the most intelligent, but the ones most responsive to change"* (Adizes, 2004).

Perhaps that's why many giants have not survived the challenges. They have not been responsive enough to changes. Take technology giants such as Kodak. They lost out because they were not responsive enough to the change of habits, desires and needs of their customers. Change and responsiveness to change are inevitable if we want to succeed.

If we want to obtain different results then we need to change something. For example, our approach, daily rituals, job, skills, dress, meal, and so on. To achieve a different result, the first step to take is to prepare for change. We cannot keep doing the same and expect a different result. The fundamental question to ask is: *"What exactly needs to be changed?"*

Do you really want to receive different results? If yes, are you prepared for change? Do you know what you are going to change? Remember, not every change is going to change your life the way you want! And you cannot change everything. I can't say it better than Jim Rohn, America's foremost business philosopher, who said: "*You must take personal responsibility. You cannot change the circumstances, the seasons, or the wind, but you can change yourself*" (Canfield, 2006).

1.2. What would you sacrifice?

We have all been there. Sometimes we need to make painful choices in our lives to move on. We love our partners, but we have concluded love alone is not enough. To achieve something greater we may have to sacrifice some great things. To hire a brilliant CEO, we need to fire a good one. The lighter our baggage the higher we can climb. Do you agree?

What are you prepared to sacrifice to achieve your dream? Imagine, you're 19, you're at the train station, you're hungry and it's midnight. You only have €3.75 cash, and the cheapest sandwich costs €3.00. You love ice-cream and you are about to hit the button on the only food machine around to buy yourself your favorite ice-cream costing €2.50. Suddenly a thought whispers in your head: "*Hang on buddy, if you buy an ice-cream you will not have enough money left for a sandwich. Are you sure you still want the ice-cream?"* Sometimes even the easiest choices may be difficult to make, but we need to make them to achieve our targets.

> *The lighter our baggage the higher we can climb.*

Assuming you want to change something to be able to do better, achieve more, enjoy more and to become more, what is it you will sacrifice? Don't worry if you don't have money as there are many ways to reproduce money if you use your talents and skills effectively. However, there is one scarce resource you must use very carefully because it is not reproducible. That's time. When it's gone, it's gone.

Many people find excuses for not doing what they want. Claiming they don't have time is a common one. But it is simple math. If you decide to spend your time watching TV, you'll have less or no time to spend on study, reading or exercise. The solution is simple but often not easy. You can't spend the same time on two things. You need to make a choice, which means you need to sacrifice something to gain something.

What is it going to be? Where are you going to find time? You spend your time watching TV, playing with your children or friends, having fun with your partner/family, working, doing personal things such as showering, sleeping, and so on. Your 24 hours is filled with these activities. Do you want to spend 30 minutes on sport/exercise and one hour on study every day? Where would you find the time? What would you sacrifice?

1.3. Find out what you're good at

To find out what needs changing, it is necessary to find out what we are born to do. It is easier to optimize from good to great as opposed to moving from poor to great. "*Everybody is a genius.*" said Albert Einstein, one of the brightest brains history has known.

I truly believe we have all been born with potential. Unfortunately, we are not always aware of what we are capable of reaching. There are many models through which we can find out what talents we have. One of them is the Wheel of Life. Are you familiar with it? If not, search for it on the web to find out more. Alternatively, reach out to <u>ImOcean Academy</u>. They will explain what it is and what you can do with this tool. While one person is good at organising the other is perfect for hospitality jobs. One is good at leading, while the other is the perfect match for innovation. What are you good at?

Ask your friends, colleagues, family and everybody who knows you well what they believe you are good at. To come to a sound list of skills you are good at also ask them why they think you are good at X. If they say, for example, you are good at planning, speaking, leading, writing, entertaining, etc., ask them what evidence they have for such an endorsement.

All successful people found out what they were good at before accelerating to the top. As an example, look at a tiny needle. If the needle is used in any other way than by its head, it will very likely be useless. However, if it is used by its head, it breaks through. How can you breakthrough? Which skill do you already have that can help you breakthrough?

Make a simple matrix of the skills. Rank the skills and select the best scoring five to ten skills. (See the exercises at the end of this chapter for a template.)

Select the best three to five which are common to the two lists and think which one makes you smile. Now take another look at the list and ask yourself which one makes you feel good when you execute things using that skill. This is probably your passion. Remember it is much easier to uplift a score from seven to nine than a score of three to seven. When you score seven on something that indicates you have talent and/or experience. Going from seven to nine will take much less energy and time than going from three to seven. The payoff for a skill on which you score nine can be phenomenal.

1.4. Find your passion

All giants who have achieved breakthrough results have had passion for what they have done. In an interview, Warren Buffett – one the of the best investors, if not the best, in history – describes his approach to work as "*tap dancing to work*". He was asked: "*How can other people learn to 'tap dance' to work?*"

Buffet said: "*Find your passion. I was very, very lucky to find it when I was seven or eight years old. You're lucky in life when you find it. And you can't guarantee you'll find it in your first job out. But I always tell college students that come out (to Omaha), 'Take the job you would take if you were independently wealthy. You're going to do well at it'*" (Buffet, 2012).

If you accelerate in your passion, you not only enjoy what you do but you may also get paid for your passion.

It is important to discover what we like to do as opposed to what we *have* to do. When we love what we do, we do it with passion. When we do things with passion we often do it well. And when we do well, we become successful. If you accelerate in your passion you not only enjoy what you do but you may also get paid for your passion. Would you agree? Remember, willingness and passion bring perseverance, and perseverance brings success.

1.5. Find a role model

Saadi (the Persian Poet 1210-1291) said: "*To do everything excellently we need to have two lives, one for trial and experience, and the other for accelerating our performance. Having two lives is impossible; the best alternative is copying best experiences of the best performers.*"

So, what would you like to become? A footballer? Then copy what Messi, Ronaldo, Maradona, Cruijff, Pele and Bekenbauer have done. Would you like to become the best *investor*? Then copy what Warren Buffet has

14

done. Would you like to become a successful entrepreneur? Then copy what people like Steve Jobs, Marc Zuckerberg and Elon Musk have done.

It is possible to become the same as your role model under one condition: doing whatever they have done. Familiarise yourself with what your role model has done. Study their biography to understand their journey to success.

1.6. Associate with winners

As quoted by Canfield, the successful business philosopher Jim Rohn famously said: *"You are the average of the five people you spend the most time with"* (Canfield, 2006).

Is this the reason that winners are attracted to winners and losers hide themselves in a crowd of losers? If you believe you are an eagle, then do not behave like a turkey. When you believe you have found your favourite field then create a list of who the most admired and successful people are from whom you can learn to move faster and smarter. Find out how you can get invited to their gatherings. Follow their strategies. Listen to their stories: how they made a billion; how they became professors; how they set up their business empire. When you have made your way to the group of the best people from whom you can learn, listen twice as much as you talk. Remember, we have two ears and one mouth. Life is giving and taking so find out how you can help these successful people. When you do so, it will be easier to ask for something in return.

When you have made your way to the group of the best people from whom you can learn, listen twice as much as you talk.

1.7. Successes follow failures

It has been said that Thomas Edison tried 1000 ways to invent the first lamp. If he had given up after the first few attempts, he would not have invented his first lamp. Next to the fact he was a genius, he is also a shining example

16

of what you can achieve with perseverance. Failures are a part of the deal. Two top teams meet in the final, one will fail to take home the trophy.

There are no better lessons than the ones we learn from our own failures. The bitterness of failure teaches us how not it does. Take the amazing story of Jack Ma (Founder of Alibaba Group) as an example. According to Forbes.com his net worth was $26.6 billion on 12-7-2016. In his interview on 29 January 2015 he said this: "*There's an examination for young people to go to university. I failed it three times. I failed a lot. So, I applied to 30 different jobs and got rejected. I went for a job with the police: they said, 'You're no good.' I even went to KFC when it came to my city. Twenty-four people went for the job. Twenty-three were accepted. I was the only guy [who wasn't].*" Ma continues as follows: "*The escrow service is about Ali pay. It was a big decision, because for the first three years we didn't do any business because there was no [way to do] payments. I talked to the banks. No banks wanted to do it. They said, 'This thing will never work.' People didn't like it. So many people I talked to at that time about Alipay, said, 'This is the stupidest idea you've ever had.' I didn't care if it was stupid as long as people could use it. Now we have 800 million people on Alipay"* (Rose, 2015).

There are no better lessons than the ones we learn from our own failures. The bitterness of failure teaches us how not to do it.

Now imagine if Jack Ma had given up because he did not have any support for establishing Alipay in the beginning. What would have happened? The same applies to us. If we do not believe in our dreams who will? If there is one person whose support matters the most when it comes to realizing a dream it is the self-support of the dreamer. We need to believe in our dream. We need to have faith in our capabilities. We need to believe the dream will result in something incredible when it comes true. So, success often comes after failure. Be persistent, consistent and believe in your success.

1.8. It's not about how hard you hit

I thought it would be worth sharing this great part of the Rocky Balboa VI movie where Rocky (Sylvester Stallone) gave the best piece of advice to his son "*Let me tell you something you already know. The world ain't all sunshine and rainbows. It's a very mean and nasty place and I don't care how tough you are it will beat you to your knees and keep you there permanently if you let it. You, me, or nobody is gonna hit as hard as life. But it ain't about how hard you hit. It's about how hard you can get hit and keep moving forward. How much you can take and keep moving forward. That's how winning is done! Now if you know what you're worth then go out and get what you're worth. But you gotta be willing to take the hits, and not pointing fingers saying you ain't where you wanna be because of him, or her, or anybody! Cowards do that and that ain't you! You're better than that!* Rocky continued: *"I'm always gonna love you no matter what. No matter what happens. You're my son and you're my blood. You're the best thing in my life. But until you start believing in yourself, you ain't gonna have a life"* (Stallone, 2006).

19

When you start your journey towards fulfilment it won't be all sunshine and skittles. There will be tough days. It may even seem unbearable at times. However, if you want to get to the finish you need to take the hits and keep moving forward. I will share practical tips to help you keep moving forward in chapters three and four.

It's about how hard you can get hit and keep moving forward. How much you can take and keep moving forward. That's how winning is done.

1.9. Find a coach

Many successful leaders – presidents, top performers and entrepreneurs – have had mentors and coaches. Bill Clinton, Andre Agassi, Serena Williams, and Richard Branson are all examples of successful people who have made it far with the help of their coaches. The entrepreneur Sir Richard Branson says: "*It's always good to have a helping hand at the start. I wouldn't have got anywhere in the airline industry without the mentorship of Sir Freddie Laker*" (Branson, 2013).

No matter how bright you are, how successful you already are, how mindful you are, hire the right coach from time-to-time and see the difference in your performance. If it helps, do it often.

Zig Ziglar, the known American author and business-man said: "*A lot of people have gone further than they thought they could because someone else thought they could*" (Ziglar, 2003).

Exercises – Chapter One

EXERCISE 1.1

Write down the answer to this question in a couple of sentences.

If you could change one thing that would have a significant impact on your life, what would that be?

The one thing I would change to significantly and positively impact my life is:

This would impact my life positively because:

EXERCISE 1.2

Decide which current activities will make place for the new activities that will help you do more, feel better and enjoy more.

Starting on [INSERT DATE], I will spend:

       hour/minutes on:

       hour/minutes on:

       hour/minutes on:

       hour/minutes on:

I will get the time I need for these activities, from the following activities:

EXERCISES 1.3

Write down a list of your skills:

I believe I am good at

because

I believe I am good at

because

I believe I am good at

because

I believe I am good at

because

I believe I am good at

because

The one thing I am very good at and I love to
do is

My network believes I am good at

because

My network believes I am good at

because

My network believes I am good at

because

My network believes I am good at

because

My network believes I am good at

because

The one thing my network believes I am very good at and I love to do is:

Make a simple matrix of the skills. Rank the skills and select the best scoring five to ten skills.

I believe I am good at:	My network says I'm good at:	What I am good at and love to do:

Select the best three to five which are common to the two lists and think which one makes you smile. Now take another look at the list and ask yourself which one makes you feel good when you execute things using that skill. This is probably your passion. Remember it is much easier to uplift a score from seven to nine than a score of three to seven. When you score seven on something that indicates you have talent and/or experience. Going from seven to nine will take much less energy and time than going from three to seven. The payoff for a skill on which you score nine can be phenomenal.

EXERCISE 1.4

Write down your passion and explain why you think this is your passion.

My passion is

because

EXERCISE 1.5

Based on your passion, find your role model and explain how you are going to become like your role model.

My role model is

I am going to do the following to become like my role model:

EXERCISE 1.6

Answer the following questions to find out whom to most associate with and why.

The five people I most associate with are:

1

2

3

4

5

The reason I associate with these people is:

Now answer the following questions:

How are these people contributing to your success?

If you continue associating with these people what will (not) change?

Who are the people you would prefer to associate with if you had no restrictions or barriers in doing so?

Why do you want to surround yourself with new people of your choice?

How can you get in touch with the people you want to associate with?

EXERCISE 1.9

Write down three reasons why you need a coach:

1. I need a coach to help me with

2. I need a coach to help me with

3. I need a coach to help me with

I will reach out to [INSERT NAME] for coaching.

Chapter 2

Keep Your Dreams Alive

"Some people see things as they are and say 'why?' I dream things that never were and say 'why not?'."

~ *George Bernard Shaw*

Why dreams matter

In this chapter, I am sharing my top tips to help you give birth to that one, life-changing dream.

Have you ever thought about why dreams matter? Do you play the lottery? Have you calculated how much you have invested in the lottery to date? Why do you do that? Just ask people around you how many of them play the lottery. I guess almost half the population does that. Why? The answer is simple. It gives them hope and a chance to dream. We invest in our dreams. When we are prepared to invest then we really expect something in return, don't we?

The question asked by many leaders I have met is: "*Do I have a great dream?*" Do you know why it matters that we believe we have a great dream? I believe because it determines how far we are prepared to go. When we believe we have a great dream, we will push ourselves to get the maximum out of ourselves. We raise above ourselves.

What is your dream? Don't make the universe wait any longer. What have you always wanted to achieve? What has held you

33

back? Why haven't you realized that one life-changing dream yet? If you don't act now, when will you?

Remember, tomorrow is not a given. Today is yours, and you can take actions which move you towards your dream. Act now. As the legendary Martin Luther King Jr. said, *"The time is always right to do what is right."*

I genuinely believe that we all have dreams. I want to take this a step further. Many of us have dreams which would change the world if they came true. Do you know why our dreams do not come true? As Colin Powell, former US Secretary of State once said: *"A dream doesn't become reality through magic; it takes sweat, determination and hard work"* (Paley, 2017).

"The time is always right to do what is right."

- Martin Luther King Jr.

If you sit back and wait for a miracle it may never happen. Dreams not followed by action may leave you feeling frustrated. Dreams are important because they play the role of our GPS (Global Positioning System). They give us direction and if we genuinely believe in our dreams we will achieve them. Trust me, all fantastic achievements start with a dream. We need to want it, we need to take action, we need to be willing to take the hits and keep moving forward and then it will happen. It may not happen as we have projected in our dreams but our lives, and probably the lives of others, will be changed.

2.1. Why people don't chase their dream

Have you ever asked yourself why you haven't taken practical steps to realize your dream? Ask yourself why you haven't. And then give a genuine answer. Many of my clients have given the following reasons for not taking action to realize their dreams:

Fear of failure

Many haven't dared to believe in their dream because they have been afraid of failure. Is this the case for you too? If yes, ask yourself what would happen if you remain afraid of failure? Nothing will change, I can tell you. If you want to realize your dream your motivation to succeed has to be greater than your fear of failure.

Lack of self-confidence

Another reason I have discovered through countless coaching sessions has been lack of self-confidence. When you are certain of things to say, you say it loud and clear. Lack of self-confidence puts you behind in everything. It puts the life you love to live out of reach. Why? It is astonishing what my clients achieve after just two to four sessions of working on their self-confidence. Their relationships are boosted, their career is much better and their finances improve tremendously. As self-confidence is a very sensitive topic we often tend to seek the reason in other things for not taking certain actions. However, digging deeper into the issues and motivations proves that lack of self-confidence is the number one reason behind many personal issues.

If you want to realize your dream, your motivation to succeed has to be greater than your fear of failure.

Limiting beliefs

An enemy that often gets in the way of our dreams, is our own limiting beliefs. *"I can't"*, *"I'm not good enough."*, *"What if I failed?"* and many more limiting beliefs come to our minds unbidden. What holds you back?

2.2. Start by writing down your dream

The first step to giving birth to your dream is writing it down *and* putting it in a place where you can see it every day. When you write your dream on a piece of paper you connect with your spiritual level. You also make a commitment to yourself. And you gradually grow into your dream. You may be aware of the power of repetition. When you repeat the same things every day, after a while it becomes habit. The same applies to your dreams. The more often you write down your dream the more you believe in it. It becomes a natural thing for you to do and you don't question it. If you haven't done this before, give it a try.

You may have doubts about taking this first step, but remember it will *take* you less than a minute. Write your dream on a piece of paper every day and always keep it with you. The power of your dream pulls you towards it.

2.3. No dreams? Who are you kidding?

Psychologists claim that more than 60,000 thoughts cross our minds every day. Some of those thoughts carry your dream. They truly do. Try it right now. Close your eyes and imagine you are in your favorite vacation place. *You* have a drink in your hand and you are sitting on a chair relaxing. The only noise which prevents you from sleeping immediately is the beautiful sound of the ocean. Now imagine you don't have any problems. You are in perfect health and you have plenty of time. What would give you a fulfilled feeling? What else would you like to achieve before departing to your final destiny? What would make you really happy?

A lottery win? Plenty of money? A much higher salary? That may be. But I believe you need to dig a bit deeper. Your dream may be something you can achieve with money. So, money is a device only. Like an airplane, which can take you to your vacation place. Make a note of what you think your dream is. Ask yourself: *"Why must I realize this dream?"*, *"How would it feel if this dream came true?"* The more you focus on your answer to the 'why', the more layers you unpack to discover your underlying dream.

The more you focus on your answer to the 'why', the more layers you unpack to discover your underlying dream.

Start dreaming NOW! And if you have one already, give birth to it. Let the world know what you want to achieve. And see what happens! I promise you, magic will happen. The universe appreciates the steps you take towards your dream. All kinds of help will come your way. You only taste this amazing experience if you take the first step.

2.4. From dream to reality

Share your dream with people you like and who are naturally supportive

Sharing your dream with supportive people motivates and strengthens your commitment to your dream. When your motivation and commitment are solid, then share your dream with people you know who will be constructively critical. You will receive consulting free of charge from these people. They can help you polish your dream and identify your challenges. They may even give you some great advice.

When you decide to chase an ambitious target, you need two types of friends:

1. Positive supporting people who say, for example, *"Wow, sounds fantastic."*, or *"What an amazing idea."*
2. People who can offer you constructive criticism.

This second group may be of even more support than the first one. They can make you think about your challenges, which helps you prepare for and avoid potential disappointments. They might also see deeper layers of your ambition which you might not have discovered on your own.

Be careful with toxic people

When you have a grand ambition, some people may laugh at you. Don't worry, that says more about them than you. Toxic people always have a problem for every solution, and only see challenges and impossibilities during your journey to your destination. They may even belittle you because they cannot see beyond a certain point. Bigger does not exist for them. Remember, you don't have to listen to everything you hear and you don't have to believe everything someone says, particularly when it comes to toxic people.

Don't think too much, take small actions instead

Many people want to think things completely through before deciding. And that's why the majority get stuck thinking about why they should and or shouldn't do something. A Persian expression says, *"A half action is worth more than hundreds of words."*

41

When you leave a motivating event, you've usually picked up some ideas about how to move to the next level. You bring your ideas home and discuss it with your partner and friends. Sometimes they support you with phrases like, *"Wow, what a great idea, you should do it, you can do it."*

A half action is worth more than hundreds of words.

However, many people often jump into the middle of your dream and create chaos for you, leaving you feeling confused. As they don't fully understand the context, and are not aware of all the ins and outs, they add more questions to those you already have. The result? You postpone your decision. And what happens when you postpone? You run the risk that it may never happen! The bottom-line: you miss another chance.

When you want to make an important decision, ask yourself one question: *"Is this the right decision to make right now?"* If the answer is yes, and you really want to achieve this, make your decision using your emotions before applying your logic to make it work. Instead of getting stuck in a closed thinking circle, take small actions. Record all the possible ways that can help you realize your dream.

2.5. Keep calm and ask for support

Please promise yourself deep in your heart that you will not let your dream die before it's even born. Giving birth to that one dream will change your life. It is crucial that you start unpacking and realizing your dream. You won't grow any plant on your own if you don't put the seed in the ground first. And then you need to nurture that seed. Start and stay committed.

If you don't know how to give birth to your dream, the best way to realize your dream is to hire a qualified coach. The coach can help you not only in the phase of unpacking your dream, but also throughout your whole journey. The right coach will not only help you to create and benefit from opportunities, but will also help you to find shortcuts and overcome challenges.

When you reach out to a qualified coach, go to him/her hungry to succeed. That way they can feed you with food to nourish your soul and mind. Then you are only steps away from realizing your dream. The right coach helps you accelerate and take the elevator to your destination.

Exercises – Chapter Two

EXERCISE 2

Write down why you must give birth to your dream:

I want to realize this dream because

EXERCISE 2.1

Now write down why you haven't taken serious steps to realize your dream. Doing so makes you aware of the reasons. As result you know what to focus and work on to change.

I haven't worked on my dream because

EXERCISE 2.2

Write down your dream using the present tense. For example: I am the CEO of multinational X, or I look great.

I am/have

EXERCISES 2.4

List the people you want to share your dream with:

1

2

3

4

List all skills you have which can help you realize your dream then select the easiest options:

1

2

3

4

List the skills you need but you don't currently possess:

1

2

3

4

Elaborate how you can learn the skills you need. Think of the people from whom you can learn, courses or trainings you can follow.

1

2

3

4

EXERCISE 2.5

Write down the coach you will reach out to, and when and what time you will do so:

I will call [INSERT NAME] on [INSERT DATE] at [INSERT TIME].

Chapter 3

Practical Steps to Realize Your Dream

"Dreams are often most profound when they seem the most crazy."

~ Sigmund Freud

What's the plan?

Every year many clients come to me with fascinating goals such as multiplying their income or starting their own business. *"What's the plan?"* I ask. *"It's in my head and I'm hoping you'll help me figure it out."* they often answer.

If you are in the same situation, allow me to congratulate you. You have already taken the first step towards navigating your way to your dream. Now you need to have a plan to make it happen. In this chapter I am happy to share practical steps which will help you realize your dream.

3.1. Promote your dream to a goal

Your journey starts when you put a date on your dream. When you have identified your dream, book an hour with yourself, for you and you only. Be as creative as possible. Think about a reasonable timeline. When do you want to realize your dream? When you do so, then your dream becomes a goal.

We can't hit the target we don't see. I believe we need to have a clear understanding of what we want to achieve. We can't say, for example, we want to grow. It is not specific enough. What does grow mean? What percentage of market share, and within what period of time? There are many models you can use to set your targets. GROW (standing for Goal, Reality, Options and Way forward) is a simple yet powerful model many coaches use to help their clients with target setting. Put a date on your dream. For example, *"By 31 October 20xx, I will have opened my Bed & Breakfast in Paris."* When you do this, you create a destination. Now you need a ticket to get there.

> *We can't hit the target*
> *we don't see.*

3.2. Imagine you have achieved your goal

Use the power of imagination to grow into your dream. Have you tried this before? Imagine your dream is $1 billion financing via an initial public offering (IPO) for your company. I can imagine how excited you are when you think about this. Now visualize it is the day you have achieved this breakthrough result. How would it feel? Are you smiling when you visualize yourself celebrating such a great achievement? Who else will benefit from you achieving this $1billion IPO? Close your eyes for a moment and imagine you are celebrating your success. It feels amazing, doesn't it? Now tell yourself that whatever another human being has done in the past has proven to be possible. So, you can do it too. Why not? Shin Sekai Yori said: "*The power of imagination is what changes everything.*" When you imagine something is possible, you are no longer stuck in the circle of impossibility, instead you enter a gear up mood.

"The power of imagination is what changes everything."
- Shin Sekai Yori

3.3. Reality check, first things first

You are now full of energy and ready to take off. You may be full of adrenaline and counting the seconds until you take a fundamental step in changing your life and probably that of others. When taking smart actions which will help you get closer to your goal, it is necessary to do a reality check. Where do you stand right now? How far are you away from your destination?

Imagine your goal is climbing Everest in two years' time. If you are a smoker (reality), you may need to quit smoking if you really want to climb Everest. One of the first smaller goals would then be: By 31 October 20xx, I will be a non-smoker.

You need an action plan to become a non-smoker. What are you going to do to achieve the goal of becoming a non-smoker? How many cigarettes do you smoke every day? When are you going to quit smoking? Frequently conduct a reality check.

3.4. Battle your limiting beliefs

They come to our mind uninvited: *"I'm not good enough." What if I failed?"*; *"How can I change my job in this situation?"*; *"I can't ask my boss. I need his support. What if he disagrees?"*; *"What if she says no?"* There are many more examples of limiting beliefs.

I believe the first, and the most important, battle we need to win is the one with our own beliefs. When we give room to our limiting beliefs, it becomes harder to get back on track. The right coach can help you with overcoming your limiting beliefs. However, by asking yourself a few questions you may reach a certain level on your own. Challenge your limiting beliefs by asking questions such as:

"How can I be certain I will fail when I haven't even tried it yet?";

"What evidence do I have that I'm not good enough?";

"Why can't I change my job in this situation?"

The first, and the most important, battle we need to win is the one with our own beliefs.

3.5. Turn 'I can't' into 'how can I?'

Instead of beating yourself up and constantly whispering to yourself: "*I can't*"; "*Why can't I?*"; "*I'm not good enough*"; "*I always fail*" etc., move yourself to a resourceful state. "*I can't*" is one of the fake havens we create for ourselves to hide from acting. Change this limiting phrase into "*How can I?*" This simple transformation moves you from a passive to a resourceful state. You become creative and think of things such as what actions you can take, and who can help you. Suddenly you hear yourself saying: "*I'll follow that great advice my grandma gave me.*"

"If you can't fly, then run. If you can't run, then walk. If you can't walk, then crawl. But whatever you do, you have to keep moving forward."- Martin Luther King Jr.

Can you recall the day you decided to take driving lessons? You knew you could not pass the driving test before taking driving lessons. So instead of sitting down and beating yourself up, you unconsciously asked yourself, *"How can I pass the driving exam?"* Then it came to you, *"Aha I need to take some driving lessons before applying to take the driving exam."* Sound familiar? You may need some support with this transformational thinking. Reach out to a qualified coach who can help you move from a frustrated to a resourceful state.

First-class leader, Martin Luther King Jr. said, *"If you can't fly, then run. If you can't run, then walk. If you can't walk, then crawl. But whatever you do, you have to keep moving forward."*

3.6. Set mini-goals followed by actions

I elaborate on this topic as I believe this step is one of the most challenging ones for many people who would love to move forward but are overwhelmed by the greatness of their challenge. Imagine your goal is to lose 30 pounds by the end of the year. Every time you think about 30 pounds it probably seems overwhelming. How on earth am I going to lose 30 pounds?

Instead of asking "*How?*" focus on your very first mini-goal. How would you feel if you aimed to lose one pound by the end of every week starting next week? It seems doable, doesn't it? You might not be able to swallow a whole cow like an Anaconda can, but you can enjoy a well-prepared steak (that is if you're not vegetarian).

3.7. Make the timelines tangible

Let's imagine you aim to achieve your dream in 10 years. What part of your dream do you want to achieve in the first two years? What will you achieve in five years, seven years...? To make it tangible and achievable, you need to think of journey goals and baby steps. What are you going to achieve in six months, three months, one month and even in two weeks? It may be too much of a stretch to have the overview now of all you need to do in the coming 10 years.

What you can do is define milestones with realistic planning. This can keep you on track. Make a close connection with your dream by committing to two-week goals and taking action to achieve those mini-goals.

Example: You want to climb Everest

Imagine your dream is to climb Everest. You turn your dream into a goal by putting a target date on it. *"In two years' time (6 October 20xx), I will have climbed Mount Everest."* The next step is to set your mini-goals. What do you need to possess to achieve your ultimate goal?

The first thing you need to be sure of is, for example, your physical health and condition. Another thing may be making sure you can devote the necessary time. If you have a job which currently does not allow you to be away longer than a week, what can you do to make time to climb Everest? What can you do to make sure you have the necessary physical condition?

The first step toward this sub-goal is identifying your current physical condition. The immediate step for achieving this goal is meeting with a professional to help you identify your current condition. The second step is setting an action plan to achieve the physical condition you need to be able to climb Everest.

3.8. Break it down into baby-steps

Thinking of the huge goal can be overwhelming. As result we make up all kinds of excuses not to act. Does this make sense? How about breaking the goal into smaller pieces from which you don't have any excuse to hide? The idea is to keep your big dream in mind while breaking it down into tangible and understandable pieces. Then you can act to realize those smaller goals. It is hard to foresee all the details that will be required over the coming 10 years. But you are capable of foreseeing the coming two weeks, aren't you? You can call your doctor to set an appointment to do a check-up. You can call your best friend to share your goal – climbing Everest – with him/her.

Remember, what we achieve at the end of the year is the sum of bits and bytes we have achieved every day.

59

3.9. Make every day count

Get up at the same time early each morning. I get up at 6.00 am every day including weekends. This gives me a disciplined structure. Every day that goes by means you have one day less to achieve your goal. Make sure every day counts. Each morning write your goal on paper noting the most important thing you're going to achieve that day. Remember, what we achieve at the end of the year is the sum of bits and bytes we have achieved every day.

3.10. Start and end your day positively

I can't emphasize enough how important it is to start and end your day positively. When you fill your thoughts with positivity you eliminate negativity. Your energy is high and you feel ready to act. When you allow negative thoughts to break in, your energy decreases and you don't feel in the mood or have the willingness to act. Regardless of whatever situation I am in, I start my day by writing the following affirmations on a piece of paper I take with me everywhere:

I am grateful

I am happy

I feel good

I love my wife and son

The first thing I tell myself when I get up is "*I am grateful*". This is also the last thing I tell myself before going to bed. This eliminates room for negative thoughts prior to going to sleep and leaves me feeling satisfied. Complaints are unable to break in resulting in peaceful nights where I sleep well. Remember, a well-rested night is a prerequisite for an energetic and productive day.

3.11. Track your progress

Keep track of your progress digitally or on paper. Imagine that you're thinking about starting your B&B in Paris. Give it a name. When you name it, you connect to it. Call it, for example, Dream Bed & Breakfast. Voila! Next register your domain name on the web. If you can't do it online, make an appointment with the relevant authorities (e.g. Chamber of

Commerce) to register your business. Then tick off what you have done already. See how motivating it is?

3.12. Never get too big for your boots

No matter how brilliant, talented, and energetic you are, never get too big for your boots. There will be days when you will feel exhausted, alone, and low fueled. Have others help you. When you feel stuck pick up your phone and call a friend or a qualified coach. Many coaches offer the first consultation for free.

Start today and take the first step of your journey. Before you know it, you will have reached your destination.

Exercises – Chapter Three

EXERCISE 3.1

Transform your dream into a goal by putting a date on it. Write your goal using the present tense:

By [INSERT DATE], I am/will have

EXERCISE 3.2

Imagine you are celebrating your success and write down what you feel:

I feel

EXERCISE 3.3

Conduct your first reality check and answer the following questions:

Where are you right now in relation to your goal? Out of 10 what score would you give yourself?

I am

I give myself [INSERT NUMBER] out of 10.

What is the first thing you need to do to kick start your goal?

The first thing I am going to do is:

I will do this on [INSERT DATE] at [INSERT TIME].

EXERCISE 3.4

Challenge your limiting beliefs by asking and answering the following questions:

How can I be certain I will fail when I haven't even tried it yet?

What evidence do I have that I'm not good enough?

EXERCISE 3.5

Imagine you want to achieve your goal but you think you can't. Turn it into how you can by completing the following:

I can achieve the goal of

by

EXERCISE 3.6

Write down the easiest actions which will help you lose one pound by the end of this week. For example, "*Starting tomorrow, I will exercise 30 minutes every Monday, Wednesday and Friday.*"

Starting tomorrow, I will

EXERCISE 3.8

Complete the following to formulate your mini-goals:

My **first** mini-goals is

and I want to achieve it by

My **second** mini-goal is

and I want to achieve it by

My **third** mini-goals is

and I want to achieve it by

Practical Steps to Realize Your Dream

My **fourth** mini-goals is

and I want to achieve it by

My **fifth** mini-goals is

and I want to achieve it by

Commit to the easiest actions by completing the following:

The first action I am going to take is

By noon tomorrow, I will have

By noon next week [INSERT DAY], I will have

By the end of the month [INSERT DATE], I will have

EXERCISE 3.9

To get the utmost out of every day, make a schedule for yourself and plot in the activities which contribute to achieving your goal.

Monday:

Tuesday:

Wednesday:

Thursday:

Friday:

Saturday:

Sunday:

EXERCISE 3.10

Write down your affirmations and leave them in a place you see frequently.

My affirmations are:

EXERCISE 3.11

Tick off what you have done at the end of every day.

I planned to do the following things:

I managed to do the following things:

Chapter 4

De-stress Your Mind and Body

"Stress is caused by being 'here' but wanting to be there.'"

~ Eckhart Tolle

Avoid stress and manage pressure

In today's world, if you wish to lead a healthy and happy life, it is essential to learn how to deal with stress. Because stress is inevitable. But the good thing is that small efforts can help you handle every stressful situation. Let's explore changes you can make to your daily regime.

Imagine there is a project deadline, an exam, or your first interview – all situations which can cause stress. Sadly, stress has become a part of our lives. A part, unfortunately, which never does our health any good.

People respond to stress differently. However, this does not mean that you cannot reduce or eliminate it. Although there's no 'one size fits all' solution for handling stress, if you feel like your life is spiralling out of control, it's high time to do something about it.

"*How are you today?*" you may ask a friend or colleague. "*I'm good, thanks for asking. Yourself?*" say some. "*Very busy nowadays*" say many. 'Busy' may be one of the most heard words in the corporate world. Do you agree? And why is that? If you feel you are too busy, have you ever asked yourself, why? Have you ever asked yourself how to manage your time and work pressure? I have been in the same shoes. And I am pleased that I have helped myself and many individuals to solve and deal with work pressure.

Stress management is something you need to learn. It will teach you healthier ways to cope with situations and will minimize the harmful effects of stress in the future.

You may be asking yourself why I incorporated this chapter in the book? Based on personal experience, and as I have heard from many of my clients, stressful days are a part of the deal. Particularly when you are on your own working toward your dream with few or no partners to brainstorm with when things get tough. To help you manage your work pressure and avoid stress a far as you can, I have included my top practical tips for keeping stress at bay below.

4.1. First, take care of yourself

Make caring for yourself a priority. If you don't, nobody else will. Learn from the security instructions given prior to flight take-offs. The flight crew tell you to secure your own mask first if there is an oxygen problem and then that of your child. I believe this is a very thorough philosophy. If you cannot breathe well yourself, you simply cannot help anybody else with breathing. So, take care of yourself. Start with eating healthily and making sure you get adequate exercise and rest.

Morning Ritual:

Start the process of 'de-stressing' as soon as the day begins. This means your morning routine needs to be changed. It will comprise of a set of actions which you take from the time you wake up to the time you head out the door. Wake up early. Yes, it might be difficult some days, but gradually it will become a habit. Welcome the 'Sun' and step out of your dwelling. In addition to all the activities you do, include a special time for meditation.

And most importantly, don't underestimate the value of these morning rituals. It gives you a perfect start to your day, which is further helpful in creating powerful momentum in your life.

Exercise Regularly:

This could be a part of the abovementioned point, but it holds a significant place in your stress management plan, and hence, I've added it separately. All highly successful people across the globe exercise regularly. And exercise is about all the physical activities which keep your body mentally and physically strong.

There's no such thing as the 'right' exercise. Choose any among the hundreds of exercises including weight lifting, cycling, a team sport, or just simply a brisk walk. The main aim is to do whatever you choose regularly. You seriously need to find a timeslot for it in your busy schedule, and ensure that you follow it.

75

The benefits are great. From increased health to maintaining youthfulness, and from enhanced productivity to assured success, it affects your life significantly.

Taking Breaks:

To do something great, you need to 'NOT DO' anything. Don't be confused! For example, you are working on a project constantly, but not getting the desired results. What do you do? You keep on trying harder, and harder, don't you? That's good, but not great. This time, try something different and take a break.

Taking breaks and disconnecting from work allows your mind and body to rest, and when you reconnect, it works better. Moreover, it offers a greater sense of control over your energy throughout the day.

Planning Ahead:

Is your day planned? No? This might cause greater stress. Setting up a time-based structure and scheduling your days in advance can simplify living. Planning makes you more productive. The reason is quite well-known; it helps you to get the most out of your day. Being confined by 24 hours each day, it is you and only you, who can work on your structural productivity. Optimizing your day proffers a real progress tracking system for your time and restores your sense of control.

Evening Routine:

Don't let your evening ruin your day. You need a wind-down routine as you move closer to the end of the day, setting you up for a fantastic night's sleep. You need to be able to forget about worries and stresses. Meditation can be a part of your evening routine. More general advice includes leaving work at work, turning off your electronic devices, maintaining a healthy diet, and sleeping soundly.

No matter how powerless you are feeling right now, these amazing ways will help you gain control over your emotions, lifestyle, thoughts, and the way you deal with problems. It is not about changing the stressful situation, it is about changing your reaction toward it!

4.2. Be proactive

Being proactive is one of most appreciated behavioural codes in the corporate world. When being proactive you often initiate your desired projects. You schedule the meetings yourself, or you give instructions to your PA to do so. Believe it or not when you take the initiative, you plan as it best suits you. For example, you consider when you have holiday plans or when your schedule is busier. This results in you reducing pressure by managing your work flow better.

4.3. Get and create clarity

Research has proven that clarity is one of the most important factors impacting performance. Make sure it is clear what you are expected to do. If you don't understand an assignment, then go to the right person and ask for clarity. How often has the following happened to you? You have done your very best but the results are not as expected. Why is that? In many cases, it's because there wasn't a clear, common understanding of the assignment and the deliverable was missing from the outset.

4.4. Have a plan

When you need to manage an initiative, or finalize an assignment, make sure you have a well thought out plan. How to start, where to start, what you need, how you can get what you need, and so on. When you have a plan, you set the plan as it best suits according to your professional judgement. When you don't have a plan, you will become a part of another's plan. Having no plans often makes you busier than you really want to be. And you run the risk of being scheduled according to other's plans, which often goes hand in hand with increased stress and work pressure.

When you don't have a plan, you will become a part of another's plan.

4.5. Learn to say No when No is best

How often has it happened to you? An important sponsor or stakeholder calls you to ask, *"Would you please do this for me by the end of the week?"* You reply, *"No problem."* Shortly thereafter you realize it is mission impossible. You feel embarrassed to let the requester know you can't meet the deadline. As a result, you feel under pressure: pressure which you have created yourself. When you can't meet expectations, simply say you can't and explain the reason. Be proactive and suggest an alternative. For example, *"Sure, I'd love to, and I could do this late next week. Is that ok?"*

4.6. Schedule to be unscheduled

Make sure you have some time every day which is yours and yours alone. It is also called scheduling to be unscheduled. I call it breathing space. Leave 10-15 minutes between your meetings to act mindfully. Even robots need to be unscheduled from time to time to maximize performance. Block some time in your agenda to work as you want to, without pressure, and at your speed. You can devote these blocks to matters which need your focus, or for brainstorming. Use a part of your unscheduled time to clear your head, go for a walk, focus or practice mindfulness.

4.7. Go to the bathroom often

Go to the bathroom a few times every day and leave your smartphone behind (if it is safe to do so). If you take your smartphone with you, do not start reading your emails and sending text messages while in the bathroom. Bathroom time can also be used as a moment to give your mind a break. If you do this, you provide yourself with regular intervals throughout the day to de-stress and to step away from any work pressure.

4.8. Don't do another's work

Should I be doing this? This a healthy question to ask yourself. Of course, we have all been helped by others on occasion. And it's good to help others when we can. But when others (colleagues or those who report to you) need your help frequently, have them learn how to fish, instead of giving them the fish every time. Help the colleagues learn to do the work instead of doing the work for them. Hire a qualified coach to help them untap their potential. Don't be a control freak, focus on results and let those who report to you work as they'd like as long as delivery is according to the plan and the company codes. Use the coaching and selling styles instead of commanding.

4.9. Skip unnecessary meetings

How many meetings have you joined which are not meant for you? Why am I here, what is my role, you may ask yourself. Skip the meetings which are not meant for you. I know a partner from McKinsey who when receiving meeting invitations always asks kindly, *"Could you please let me know what we will be talking about? I'd like to prepare."* When not sure, just ask: what is the purpose of the meeting?

4.10. Read and answer emails in one go

I spoke with one of my executive clients who receive around 500 business emails per day, excluding text messages. He said he allows two slots per day in his agenda to read and answer his emails. He quickly scans his emails for several criteria, e.g. subject, urgency, sender and relevance. He forwards the emails to his team members based on subject matter.

Personally, I put my CCs[1] in a separate box and read them three times a week. If I am the person to act, then I act accordingly. Make sure you do not open several emails simultaneously unless they are interconnected. Sometimes you get involved in an escalation

---

[1] CC means carbon copy. Carbon copying someone on an email is a great way to keep them in 'the loop' and allows them to know what is going on without being involved. These are copies of the emails sent to the main recipients. The unwritten rule is that CC means you are not the main person to act. However, not everyone agrees with this rule. You may still receive a CC and be expected to take action.

or exciting discussion, which can distract you from the task at hand. It's easy then to close your mailbox having forgotten to read and answer the mails as you intended. As a result, you will receive embarrassing reminders, which will only escalate work pressure and stress.

4.11. When you are free, stay free

Manage your work during your work time so that you don't have to work during your free time. When you work during your free time, you cannot rest properly, and you don't spend enough quality time with your loved ones. You may find yourself mixing work and private life. The issues on either side impact the other. After a short while you feel a huge pressure. When you are stressed and under pressure, you cannot perform at your best. This in turn exacerbates work pressure and stress and you may find it encroaching increasingly on your private life. As a result, work pressure and stress may lead to a burnout.

4.12. Find out critical success factors

Not everything matters and you need to focus your time on that which does. When you have many things on your plate, create a common understanding with your team and stakeholders about what is important and what isn't. Get clarity on the key success factors[2]. Focus on the 20% of the activities or initiatives which represent 80% of your performance or success. Find out when the assignment is due. Remember, it's a short distance between success and failure.

4.13. Work smart, play smart

Instead of working hard and playing hard, work and play SMART. Make sure what you do is **S**pecific, **M**easurable, **A**chievable, **R**elevant and **T**ime related. By working SMART, you won't spend endless time on

---

[2]The combination of important facts that is required in order to accomplish one or more desirable goals. For example, one of the key success factors in aircraft industries is safety. If the aircraft is not safe enough bankruptcy is inevitable.

never-ending initiatives that don't have a clear road map and predefined deliverable. To me, playing smart means doing things we enjoy the most within our allocated resources (i.e. time and money). When you have an hour-long conversation with your partner, don't reply to the distracting messages coming from all kinds of apps. Be fully present so that you have an enjoyable and fruitful discussion.

4.14. Develop and use your soft skills

Research has proven that almost 85% of what we achieve is thanks to our soft skills.

As quoted by Sally Hogshead *"Forbes magazine reported research findings that indicated that 85% of your financial success is due to skills in 'human engineering' your personality and ability to communicate, negotiate and lead. Shockingly, only 15% is due to technical knowledge"* (Hogshead, 2014).

I believe we have failed in many cases due to shortcomings with our soft skills. So, refresh your soft skills such as communication, relationship management, listening and sensitivity. Just ask your stakeholders, your manager, sponsors, and your colleagues what they appreciate the most and what you should avoid when engaging with them.

4.15. Top secrets may not be secure forever

We live in a time in which teenagers can hack highly secure systems and gain access to top secret information. Over the course of time, many secrets become public – planned and unplanned. There should be a good balance between risk and reward. Is the reward worth the risk? If you take the risk, bear in mind that it may become public someday. How bad would it be if your secret became public? If it became public, how great would the pain, shame and potential damage be? It's worth thinking more than twice when taking certain risks. Remember, technology does not always work in our favour: instead of traditional trusted hard copies, almost everything is digital nowadays. When something is digital, we can never be sure it is 100% secure. Avoid unnecessary stress by taking calculated risks. If you can't bear the consequences of a secret becoming public don't have secrets which you will be ashamed of if they are made public.

When something is digital, we can never be sure it is 100% secure.

4.16. If it doesn't feel right, it is not

We've all been there. Things come along which don't seem to be quite right. When we listen to our intuition it says don't do that. In many cases, if it doesn't feel right it is indeed not right. Decisions that are ethically wrong are being taken by some leaders every day. It will not remain sunny all the time. One day it may get cold. It may snow or rain heavily. You better be prepared. If you get an offer which seems too good to be true, find out what's on the other side of the coin. If you accept an offer which may bring your integrity into question, do so with the knowledge that it may become public someday. If you believe you can live with the consequences, then accept the offer. But if you believe your reputation would be ruined if it becomes public, just don't do it. Committing to things which do not look right brings a lot of unnecessary pressure and stress.

4.17. Never feel too big to ask for support

We're human. Sometimes we're mentally and physically at our best and sometimes we're not making the best decisions. When you don't feel comfortable about something, reach out for support; consult a trusted adviser or book a couple of sessions with a qualified coach. By enlisting the support of an adviser or coach, you'll gain precious insights that will help you make better decisions.

Exercise – Chapter Four

EXERCISE 4.17

Answer the following questions:

What are the 3 things that cause the most stress for you?

1

2

3

What are you going to do to manage your stress?

1

2

3

I am going to take the following actions:

1

by [INSERT DATE] at [INSERT TIME].

2

by [INSERT DATE] at [INSERT TIME].

3

by [INSERT DATE] at [INSERT TIME].

Final word

Have you ever thought about the dream life you would like to live? What would it look like? What holds you back from living your dream life? Ask yourself what have you done so far to give birth to that one important dream? What have you done before to achieve other goals? What has worked and what hasn't? What would you do if you knew you couldn't fail? What are you without realizing that one life-changing dream? How happy are you now? I can ask you many more questions which may spike your adrenaline and make your heart work harder. The point is that you must become conscious of the precious time you have now to give birth to your dream. If you keep waiting for a miracle, I'm afraid it may be wishful thinking. While hope is a very beautiful and important thing in life, I'm afraid isn't a strategy. If you want to do better, become more and achieve more, you need to move out of your comfort zone.

Nobody else may be interested in you achieving your dream. How about you? Do you really care about your future, your fulfilled life, your ultimate success, and your happiness? If you do, find out what makes you feel fulfilled, happy and loved. Many of us have been kidnapped by money, by the luxury of strategic positions at great organizations. Many of us have been kept in prison by money. We build virtual unbreakable walls around ourselves by chasing money. I know what I am talking about because I've been there.

There have been years in my life where I worked like an idiot until midnight or beyond. I even enjoyed it. I was chasing money for an extravagant lifestyle; a better car, a bigger house, a luxury vacation. The truth is that while I became more successful every year, I didn't become happier. I was doing great things but I didn't enjoy them due to the stressful walls I had built around myself. I only awakened when I hurt physically feeling pain in my shoulders and hands. That's when I asked myself if this would ever be the right thing. I had sacrificed my health for a promised tomorrow which might never come. What is the point of spoiling now for later? Would I be healthy enough to enjoy the wealth I was chasing?

My tipping point came in 2011. Since then I have developed myself as far as I have been able to. I discovered the spiritual world which feels like a warm bath for me. First, I found my passion: coaching. I have realized the more people I help to achieve their goals and realize their dreams the more fulfilled I feel. Zig Ziglar was right in saying: *"You can have everything in life you want, if you will just help enough other people get what they want."* I've helped many clients who were slaves to money or their jobs. They had money and were successful, but they were unhappy. Some were even on the edge of suicide. I have helped couples who were just a step away from divorce rediscover their relationship.

Do you want to know how? It is all in the mind. You become what you believe as Oprah Winfrey says. Don't chase the money. Don't follow any path blindly. Find out why you were born. Find out what your destination is supposed to be. Find out what destination makes you feel good when you imagine you're already there. Find your passion. When you do what you really love, you do it well. When you do it well you may even get paid for that. And you will be happily doing what you enjoy. Then you will be both happy and successful living your dream life. Chase your dream, and I will see you at the top.

Gifts for you

References

Adizes, I. (2004). *Managing Corporate Lifecycles: How to Get to and Stay at Top.* Santa Barbara, California, U.S.A: The Adizes Institute Publishing.

Branson, R. (2013, November 25). Richard Branson: the importancen of a business mentor. *www.virgin.com.*

Buffet, W. &. (2012, November 26). Tap Dancing to Work. (C. Rose, Interviewer) CNN Money.

Canfield, J. (2006). *The Success Principles: How to Get from Where You Are to Where You Want to Be.* U.S.A: HarperCollins Publishers.

Hogshead, S. (2014). *How World Sees You: Discover Your Highest Value Through the Science of Fascination.* New York, U.S.A: Harper Business.

Kelly, M. (2004). *The Rhythm of Life: Living Eeveryday with Passion & Purpose.* U.S.A: Beacon Publishing.Paley, N. (2017). *Leadership Strategies in the Age of Big Data, Algorithms, and Analytics.* Florida, U.S.A: CRC Press.

Rose, C. (2015, January 29). Charlie Rose Talks to Alibaba's Jack Ma. *Bloomberg*.

Stallone, S. (Director). (2006). *Rocky Balboa VI* [Film].

Ziglar, Z. (2003). *See you at the Top: THE "How To" book that gives YOU a "Check Up from the "Neck Up" to eliminate the "Stinkin Thinking" and AVOID "Hardening of the Attitudes".* Gretna, Louisiana, U.S.A: Pelican Publishing Company.

About the Author

Hamid Safaei has a deep passion for creating a better world full of better leaders.

He is a certified executive coach best known for helping people make breakthroughs in Leadership, Personal Success and Conflict Resolutions. Through his coaching, Hamid has helped his clients awaken their 'why', giving birth to their underlying dreams.

Hamid loves helping other individuals discover the best version of themselves. He regularly posts blogs on his website at https://ImOceanAcademy.com on subjects including personal life, leadership, realization of dreams, stress, target-setting, decision making, and unleashing potential.

Hamid is an expert at balancing his professional and personal life, a man who works very hard but still makes it home in time for dinner with his wife and son almost every evening.

About First-Class Leadership

First-Class   Leadership is a comprehensive book that all managers and leaders should read. The amount of information is second to none. A brilliant book based on research and experience brings to the fore everything you need to know about being a first-class leader.

The techniques and advice in this book are simple yet effective, and when you read them, you will wonder why you never thought of doing them before. In *First-Class Leadership*, Hamid Safaei covers everything from getting people to believe in your vision; building effective teams; communicating, inspiring, encouraging, and developing employees so they give their very best; caring and nurturing your workforce; to finding and keeping talent that will take your company to the next level.

This book will change your perspective on how leaders should lead and how managers should manage. Taking inspiration from icons such as Gandhi, Gates, Musk, and Jobs, what Hamid Safaei brings together is a wealth of information that will pave the way for everyone to become a first-class leader. This is a book that everyone should read!

www.ingramcontent.com/pod-product-compliance
Lightning Source LLC
Chambersburg PA
CBHW050457290526
45786CB00006B/2331